Stil Cagey

Stil Cagey

Sebastian Schloessingk

GOMETRA

© Sebastian Schloessingk 2021
Cover Painting © Alba Lydia
Schloessingk 2021
Frontispiece by Robert
Gibbings © NCB 1939
Printed and bound
in Great Britain
by IngramSpark
Set in Adobe
Garamond Pro on
18/12/25
by Roc Sandford at
the Gometra Press
a sister imprint of Soho

ISBN 978-0-948166-24-2

For Iona, Alba Lydia and Ottilie

Table of Contents

11/16   1
Boy Own Progress   2
The Advent of Kleenex   4
White Girl S.E. Asia Leg   5
Reversible   6
Flipper Beach   7
They Know Where   9
Hand-weighed   10
Looking Both Ways   11
Hitherto Unassuming   13
A Romp Through   14
Attitude Passé   16
Laminata   18
Party Isle   19
Mudhut, Walnut, Drone   20
Bedside Apple   22
Winter Olympics   23
Nordic Hi   24
Interbrokered   25
Upcurling   26
One Alley   27
Rug Ridge   28
Showing The Door   29
To Be Of Help   31
Gallantry Bundle   32
Stop, Look Up … and Seal   33

Flection   34
Honest Years   35
An All-Star Reception Er When   37
Within Reach   38
Comets Meteors Eras   39
Stranger Warmth   40
Now descends the …   42
Far From How   43
A Crab Steps In   44
What's This?   45
Our German Guest   47
Cry Of The No-No   48
Monochrome Gig   50
Gamut   51
Over And Over Again   52
Hoisted   53
Jetties Out   54
Scaredy Cusp   56
Virtuoso Drum Roll   57
Incautious Pluck   58
Anemone of the Evolved   59
Cow Motif   60
Oscillatory   61

11/16

I finished breakfast, having had enough.
And slid the bowl and muesli grouping
a little away, in sign. It was a
minute or two before it trickled
through, what I'd had enough of: the vicious
turns of events laid out, laying waste
longstanding hope across the world. Events
which in worst case after case had boiled
up on each other and overshat the limits
of stimulus, readership, news.
I resumed breakfast, print nourishment
taken (inseparable?) with it *again* –
or a craven sullen no platform
newsless surface (can't remember which) –
the milk level in the translucent plastic
clear on the point, I had *not* had enough.

Boy Own Progress

Men's inner city muscle gym *leg days*
are rumoured to be much shirked.
Everyone wants the pecs, sleevebustout
biceps. Anyhow legs are known to
be less responsive (and calves often not

at all) to the onslaught of the laggard
sweating self in the pavement-peer-through
glass dungeon of machines ... 'That boy's
a bit fat' – I indicated
a small figure with gibbous armour

in a CBBC animation.
'No, he's not!' the reply, shot back.
'He's a knight. Knights are never fat.' ...
Cage-fighting, kik-texting, where it was at.
There'd been a step-up in stabbiness

too, whereby the usual 2D
Loser! sneer – launched at the hapless
with index and thumb at 90º –
got a third dimension L blast via
the middle finger. Hand usage, ever

developing: no actioner,
no thriller would dream of someone
checking the pulse of someone motionless
as formerly at the wrist. Has to be,
for the gumshoe citizen (muscle bulk

tamed by coat) down on one knee, lightly
the finger pair to the side of the throat
of key players found streetfallen, desk-slumped …
'I was like *result.*' This from boy walking just
behind in the dark of the cold fortified

people stream skirting a Samuel-Palmerish
church, quitting the field of fireworks. To cap
his meticulous 'I was like', 'She was
like' account of a conversation
(or stichomythia) with.

The Advent of Kleenex

Those with long memories reach
for the hanky. 'So useful under
the bonnet.' Slowing jam, A23,
gradual vindictive and overheating
breakdown. Up flips the bonnet, out
whisked without ceremony the cotton

hanky from the trouser pocket.
A white lifebelt for the boiling hot
radiator cap predicament. Slung
round, smothers, unscrews with a strong
hand, it's a hissing start. Moreover
those with short memories have

taken to forgetting their mothers'
birthdays in every land. Seeing
as you can't put a knot in a Kleenex
very well. Nor tie and hang four
in a wispy tissue to ward
the frigging sun off your bonce

on a shoulder of A23, any more
than you can keep other cars' moony
passenger faces from completing
the entire rotate-and-stay-with angle
one by one. You've nothing to say them
but pissed off and can't give up.

White Girl S.E. Asia Leg

For Iona

The impression in Thailand, Laos, Cambodia,
was Slim Buddha sits, gold-leafed, in each
temple. Whilst in China and Vietnam

Fat Buddha held sway, if anything the more
perfect for it. And sometimes repose would be
for Buddha only. *Don't "sit" here please*

one temple stipulated, with
an easy mastery of post-modern layering.
More solicitous in outreach

was the Bangkok Royal Palace sign *Do
not trust wily strangers.* Spoken as if
already squatting down alongside, arm

round shoulder but so not wily. Rather
intimate again, but less wordy,
a local woman's opener on the beach:

fingerpoint-straight, she said *'Hairy'.* ie
your legs (no Buddha's) could do with the
depilatory arts of a 'threader' like her.

Reversible

Babies don't mind faces and eyes
upside down, leaning over them.
Whereas it spooks the downlooker,
and exiles baby eyes that beam

affection in trusting reptilian
shape, or sci-fi lidding.
Even more unsettling than
the sly sea-going reversible

bearded Dutch sketch-captains of old.
Also, toddlers find tickling
an unmixed pleasure, the more relentless
the better – whereas for us on

our backs the torture component,
the torture interpretation,
grows as life proceeds, till now
it's totally uppermost.

Flipper Beach

We get tanned – or conceivably burnt – the more
on the left of the body in the Northern
Hemisphere. Having arrived at midday or
a while after lunch on beaches of the west
coasts of islands (or nations), looking forward

to a generous run of sun into sea. Across
the sand a snorkeller, with outstretched footwear
and the deep aims implied, made flipperprint tracks,
herringbone progress to water, not dainty, mask
pushed up top, but longer the flipper, as you're aware,

the more expert the diver. Just as the longer
the skis that once climbed in Kneissl isolation
above the cable car's every-way-gazing
hemmed upright bunch, the more godlike the short (strong
calves, jersey, and snowglared an exotic brown)

instructor: off-piste gullies and vistas waiting,
free day, glove his, light grip. Here instead – it's *jet skis*
beyond the swimmer diaspora barely,
flat-bouncing and raising a bird-of-paradise
plume behind them, squirted water deftly put.

The diver, impassive at mid-depth holding out,
had logged the topography (sand, rock) rumple
of seabed into octopus, and back into
no such story. Causing my partner, her silhouette
clarifying elbow-propped, to retrieve a fact:

octopuses keep a few braincells farmed out
along the tentacles. Man has, I said, somewhat
darker side roused and affably turned, a thinking
tentacle too, with braincells enough for one
thought only. Upon which I stood up, strolled the damp

gleam ribbon (smoothed by the waves' volte face),
traversed by a sense of each walking swimmer.
Cellulite matrons, burdening black costumes. Pallid
young gamma male in lonesome speedo. Plashed-up
tummies stepped pensive, hand in hand. A thirty-something

gaunt of bikini was approaching, past a family
all of whom obese, all present cloudless happy
in the spume. And what about when that tentacle
of squeezed creative thought can grab itself genetic
back-up, remix, the *alpha menu* beckons? Was this

the last golden epoch of wholesale ferocious
human variation, from the ideal? Before
the 5'10/6'3 slender brainy natural
blondes and blonds, quick to arise, slow to age, pack out
the 2050 beach paseo, inclined to blank me.

They Know Where

In early days they'd have the jungle – albeit
high-end studio jungle – or some other form
of gulp-pitted wilderness, crag and shadow stain,
to provide an eery setting in a film.
Scary wilderness much later rebranded,
emerged: post-industrial wilderness. Sewers
of lovingly built dripped-through Victorian
nether-city brick vaulting in its might, entropic
factories, inaudible railway waiting-rooms lopped
(the old papers chucked, floor displeasing). And halls of machines
unwieldy with foreboding (opaque as to founding use), mildew
labs, warehouse cagelifts jolted anew and by whom ... Here
thrillers went (or snow-gruel Scandis) – to the bruised locations.

Hand-weighed

My head flattened my hand
as my hand cradled my head.
Every night, with a view to sleep.
My hand showing spirit
flexed without notice, and
raised my skull a couple of inches
off the sheet or edge of pillow.
For once the neck muscles
left out of the loop, the matchless
power steering of the neck
('Forget your Weight of Head')
lay idle. Very heavy
and very hard, was the report
from fingertips splayed and poised.
Feel the full weight and
you feel the full hardness.
'Hard fucking head' went the head
in an undertone in the dark.
Anyway unheard by
the human dense genuine
in the vicinity unseen
across the night sheet earplugged.

Looking Both Ways

On the front of The Culture
section (a Sunday) was Leonard Cohen
looking good. And deep and sufficient in
the face and green-eyed at the age
of 80 or so. Tipped forward – in his
case allowably – the Trilby
he favours. (As do stars and rockers
ageing around the world specially

for interview: with Fedora, black or slate
Trilby – denoting *still cool* – they face down
the grotesque, not me baby.) And
beneath was printed, not quite him,
I intend to live forever.
Culture's back cover monopolized
meanwhile by Phil Collins looking *bad,*
pottering-smiley and skimped with age.

Next to *him* was printed more rueful than wise
NOT DEAD YET, not 100%
rescued by the framed (line-encoffined)
pay-off pun LIVE! (at the RAH).
The one remotely youth thing
a vague insert of grizzled chin stubble
which had to do, didn't. However
L.Cohen's photo as it transpired

may not have been super-recent
and that statement of intent, whether his
or tweak of journo, provoked matters
in the purest fashion. He, of the two

the evergreen, a few weeks on (it happened
this time to the whole of him) was dead.
He passed as 'ugly' in his pull-no-
punch lyrics, more like photogenic.

Hitherto Unassuming

We were trying to locate Easter, often something
of a query, on the fridge-attached calendar.
Nothing doing. Calendar too PC. Cosying up
to the high ground vacated, I spoke of my mother
having made, possibly twice, the Crowpatrick

pilgrimage. She might I acknowledged have done
part of the ascent by bus. And any pilgrims advancing
over the scree toward the summit on their knees
(a knot of snails in their purposefulness
converging) could well involve kneepads. A sterner

tone: the *Go and Sin no more,* rammed across
the whitewash above a door lintel of English/
Welsh village church, for centuries upbraiding and
invigorating. Till abruptly in the selfsame
black script, which didn't mess, *Go out and Sing more*

was the edict, a rethink smuggled in with po-
faced painterly skill (and a nod from the) ... Obvious, one
has to resist suchlike slippage, with Might and Main.
Also the conclusion after a logical study
of endless co-incidences, girding round one's life

and starkly implausible, mounting over time, circling
in, padding in towards the Crowpatrick of this
unassuming mere fact noter, that oneself (of
all people), pushing back one's chair, is probably God.
An insight taken in One's stride (sort of deflating).

A Romp Through

The world was jaunty –
'Here's looking at Euclid!'

But then the turn
of Flat Earthers and Wide

Berthers sent to
snuff the light. Music brought

some relief, the Partita
in Paracetamol.

German materialist
philosophers weighed in

as boxers do, and waited
for the Ding. Sexual

things gnawed the clergy, viz.
The Ordeal of Kilvert Girlpin.

For bands of Wandering
Menstr'ls, the vote was the grail.

At last the First World War
over, the worst furled away.

The troubles marking time
in Co. Interim.

Eventually the
individual even

dented China and
did it m'ai Wei.

Attitude Passé

The wavering bonnet-aerial proved
a lightning rod for birdshit.
Until, loose in its socket,
it slid down to the side lying back
like an unpredictable animal ear

and whipskimmed stray pedestrians.
Rule: overtaking is only
forgiven if and when you
overtake the next car too.
Which draws, textbook, the sting.

I myself smile on the faster
car overtaking, or nicely
slow down (similarly
at dinner parties yielding the
ultra-throaty car – yet louder mouth –

the floor, safe passage, wave them on).
Sometimes it's a biker, exhaust
lodged oddly high, blasting
outer anus between numberplate
and seat, that passes (or oncoming

police car that flashes alternate
headlights – child learning to wink).
A long and tough journey's
speeding completed, I could easily
lean down and pat the tremble

-rippled lathering flanks of
the mileage-heavy car. I carefully
grimed its numberplate for a year,
resisting the Sunday wash
with fortitude. I met my match

in a speed camera as dourly dirty.
Who'd win – both on a skulk-yellow
grime caper – was down to the photo
finish. I knew a Civil War
re-enactor (roundhead) whose

BMW was ornamented
with – safer bet – a trap-detector,
pleasing bulky dashboard extra
(and whose wall with double costume
portrait). Other drivers have gone

for shiny free-gliding radial hubcaps
given to purling backwards like stagecoach
wheels, and addling you to the brink
of jumping the lights. They've lent 'I think
I'll take her for a spin' new frisson.

Laminata

She slipped her torso between
the upper bars of a field gate,
wedged it there more or less balanced
and practised breast-stroke legs
in the layer of air. Said was the thing
to do, coming up to holidays
by the sea. I wouldn't be surprised
if, in *most* of the gates we now
encountered, a swimmer wasn't
practising, I agreed. That – her wrist
debated – could be going too far.

She got a heavy cold. I was asked
to apply to her chest the Vicks
Vapo Rub. I did, disturbed
by the aftertrace on my sight
of her torso thinness, the taut casing.
Children often having not much
leeway above the self pack.
Might this even tamper with
the lamination sequence? So little
margin in fleshing out from the bone
one being and her range of jokes.

Party Isle

Where was 'Eye Beefa'? It is
the party isle. Airport and sea
of arms shoaled up
zenith. Favour one hip,
and biceps boy guns
make female guns legs.

Laserwork, E's, lagers. Sea shacks
and the meandering shingle girl. 'Like
some fish?' 'Ish.'

Mudhut, Walnut, Drone

In the odd mudhut first to show up was
TV, then mobiles, solar panels on
their way. American anchorwomen were
so dated – the perm, the screenworthy
pink-over skin, the middle/elderly
smile-grooved fossilness. Should they consider
wearing dresses of meat? There ensued
an ugly metal flare-up from somewhere

about Madonna's face, on view
at a media event. Enjoy – if not
an outing here for a soigné airy
feminizing garment of hers – the *grills*
spiked in or moulded, hammered on (to confer
cutting edge). Or take in a May Day Red Square
parade through which, under commentary,
rolled *the Iskander family of weapons,*

Cruise-type on flat trailers, speaking for
themselves. That a family nowadays
can be a family of weapons, wow.
And through *Naples* will roll, should Naples
ever apocalyptically
succumb, the lava. *Or* the rubbish.
Uncollected, towering, squirming round
the corner of rough quartiere, palazzo.

Not discreetly out of sight at all, as in
a modest hired Audi the discovered
radio/CD player was – let deep
into the glove box back wall. Recalling

behind twin walnut cabinet doors
the honeymoon of the living-room telly.
Along with one BEA Comet, beyond
and between the curtains. Become so full

of jet bray the sky, if soon it's latticed too
with drones, legal low over the garden
hedge-hopping, chunky, or *(AI)* bee-size, I'll go
ballistic (and pierce on up).
But to tell of our actual flight, and the aisle
offerings, there arrived in due course a phase
of turbulence and Perfume by Beyoncé.
When the beat drops, the wonk *comes in.*

Bedside Apple

Particular women who swallow their cheeks
without hesitation for mirrors ... The real
smell of a person, is it their breath, dry skin, sweat

or that which enables you to note who was last
on the toilet? Myself, when I sneeze I smell of
my father. Blow your nose in a kleenex,

you print off an elusive butterfly of snot.
And *'My thighs have grown overnight,'* she complained
who complains so much I recommended she wear

a stiff body-non-viewing ruff. Like the inverted
(head-non-scratching) cones on park dogs spotted.
'I know you think jerky is the way forward,'

she'd cautioned earlier, by then met with a snore.
Don't snore it seems when she clasps me, from behind.
(Is the snore a cry for love? And a hug merely what

keeps you off your back?) In the wan morning
I woke, reached for an apple, bit on it and broke
mid-bite into the snore and sleep of a sucking pig.

Winter Olympics

On the whole Britain doesn't hold its snow any
more (as certain men don't hold their liquor).
The Scottish Ladies' curling team's previous
success, though, means we're obliged to watch them for hours.
The grossly boring absurd low single-kneed intense
slide onward behind the kettlish thrust. Ahead of which
feverish (toothbrushlike) cross-brushing. Intense in
its own right, our close-up – on the agonistic
face – pulls back at a locked distance, camera

crew retreating on ice knees as gruellingly
committed no doubt. More absorbing for some
are half-naked Chinese female skaters ('They look
green on ice,' spoke up an unjaded eye). And among
the Pairs highlights, a *Bottomsniffer Spin* –
each bent supple on an elegant skate, with head
to partner's rear ... Somerset House does its bit,
throws its annual booked-out (evocative
of the Thames Fairs) family romp-rink down, bluelit.

Nordic Hi

In a horn of sunlight above the lake or fjord
a quiet mound of several fields. The family opted
to head back to our car but I continued on
the little road or track, and saw a bare-chested cyclist
moving gradually up the far side of the rise

towards me. As he drew level, collar-length brown
well kept hair, tanned sinking moobs, I gave a brisk 'Hi!'
He answered with a searching glance and a drawled
'Hi!', suave but plaintive. Soon afterwards I peered
back and captured him havering over the brink

of the rise, black-torsoed against the shine of fjord,
fiftyish, German or French, it would seem
gay and riding off a touch disconsolate
into the sun, on his solo cycling
holiday, as lonely as in a folk tale woodcut.

Interbrokered

At the wealthy end of the range, mature
leaders and candidates with momentum felt
impelled to bound up the one or two steps
to the rostrum, in a sprightly moribund
semblance of youthful acceleration

on their suited way to the waiting mike.
At the other end of the range, worldover
in sandy or dusty or leafy terrorist
cabins, shapely pin-ups still posed tacked
to the wall: Kalashnikov diagrams

with underneath not 38-26
-38, but 9-11-01 superscribed
on specifications, directions for use
carefree and tatty ... In between stood,
mediating, American soldiers 'passing

wind in front of tribal elders', a charge
aired in a report suppressed (but not). More
mediating: conferences, where such
was my crude urge to guess and blurt it, were
I rashly allowed in the auditorium, not

one of the ponderous slowmo new-speakers,
pausing (ever since George Schultz) to make
with diverse stakeholders significant eye
contact, would get to finish the sentence
themselves, for all their statesmanlike cluster-mikes.

Upcurling

The dead ewe wore a costly head-dress
of bluebottles, lustrous chain mail, no chinks.
There's a sunset flush on the drowned retrieved

newt belly, spattered with greater
and lesser ink planets. In common: farm
animals, men wherever, women, all *cough*

the same. And our living sculpture tree – so
called because it's dead and branch parts drop
off in the wind, ever changing the cherry's

truncated form … Is that a tractor,
lancetip to ground, lunch in cab or is it
Don Quixote notion-struck in a hedged field?

And then her just observation: the grey-
skinned upcurling twig ends of an ash
each beckoning 'like E.T.'s finger'.

One Alley

To be back in a world, a *city* (smaller than many
a Chinese 'village' of now) with the oldest building
the biggest, the dusty temple down one alley
the colossal thing (not some – glint-subdued – superlative
Bank Tower), and simple beige or warden dusk mountains beyond –
is the reverie. More recent, a 3500-

year-old Egyptian surface scrawled on by tarrying boy
who bequeathed amid hieroglyphs his name in Chinese.
Photographed and uploaded onto the internet by
a fellow countryman who'd tried and failed to efface it,
the tourist-abroad defacement was bewailed by countless
Chinese as national shame and loss of face.

In London a brief scrawl of type commissioned for
the tucked-away art show – a prose bounced up on the wall
with the artworks – was described on the phone by its author
(part of an artwork?) as more a 'standalone fragment', little
read. The asker, who had though, was moved to cite
Ozymandias's 'standalone ruin' ... Far from standing

alone, 100 million more Chinese to be levered
off the countryside into agglomerated
tower blocks, graphite of hue, dull jagged. This the intention,
hope and a prime element of the official radiant
'Chinese Dream', promulgated by the new leadership.
The work (the gift) of urbanization *is far from complete*.

Rug Ridge

Jets confining themselves to the vapour trail
of the one before, like sheep to a spindly well-marked
(if slightly less straight) dirt path over a grass field.
Jets and their fleece path. Below, orange-fly-on-black-
faeces-of-sheep season. The specialist monochrome
tawny orange flies on each plump drying fissured length.

Elsewhere a hoover drove a rug ridge before it, much
like a fur fold along a dog's back forcefully stroked.
Among the few wild creatures prepared to play, flit
with us, in and out of the dark wood, is a robin.
Which, at (crude) table, hopping for muesli cairn-scraps,
found we're about big jet (from tarmac) size. Maybe board
and sit six abreast in our fuselage, six redbreast.

Showing The Door

In homely vein looking around
or looking ahead, there may be talk
in company or sole musing
of *getting through* old age. Until
realizing, 'chillingly', there is
no *through* because there's no other side.

The last of sleep, and a dream fragment
where I was a teenager in short.
Waking, and an awareness hissing in
that actually – which I did mention
within the dream tail, or *to* the
dream candidly – I was more than

a teenager now. Already grown-up.
What, 20s or so? Perhaps more.
I had to prod the bar higher and higher
through each decade in fresh-faced good faith,
taken aback, incredulous and slowly
dismayed to the point of feeling sick.

In the end a skeleton is the thing
to be. Or no? 'Three out of four' (in Britain,
was it) 'choose cremation'. The urban
choice. For brute fadeout, and fleeing
the desecration and bulldozed upheaval
in store for graveyards in cities (graves thrust

under carparks, crooked not spared) ... Burial
at best: a church-and-yew-shade rural
solace. Especially for anal

retainers. The skeleton 'hoarded'.
In a low-lying drawer like everything else was.
Yet when the bony figure in black

Death's hood came to overnight, what did
the man who would live an incalculable
age abrasively whisper?

'Go, Figure.'

To Be Of Help

Autobahn Kapelle, read the motorway sign,
blue, and gestured into the pines, spruce. For the pious
German artic-driver or Porsche-owner a break,
a refuge, a chapel set a short way back
in passing forest gone banal (depleted
of tall shield spirits, and Roman-loathing eyes).

On a lengthy autobahn trip north to south
two cars, unacquainted, overtook each other
in turn, in due course, without exasperation,
a species of mutual succour, relieving
each other of the tedium – and lead – like team
cyclists in a two-man windbusting row.

And the heavy dark oblong projecting branch
of information gantry, implausibly wielded
by one post (though thick), bore nothing but the time
digital, composed of a handful of coppery dots
dwarfed, the bulk an unused gunmetal grey. All there
was to convey? Worth putting? Or was it the grimmer

(in Times New Roman) for being put? As backseat
to front, of a car delving at peer speed through
under Time's dotted monument, the question
'What's a convent?' travelled. Adult pause. And the not
wholly unpious but historically
hapless answer, 'A place where you pray, and yeah ...'

Gallantry Bundle

Girl at rest alongue a (scuffed) chaise longue,
or 'chaise lounge' as an Essex
auctioneer had it. I offered her
'a small ghostly egg dish'. She said what,
I said 'a phantomlet'. The ghost sloped off
into the wide world with just a flimsy
bundle on his memory stick.
There he saw Ladies before Gentlemen,
pearls before swine. Genuine style
gallantry too. What does a cowboy
send out to his sweetheart when he's in
a romantic mood? Posse of flowers.
How did Brezhnev comport himself
with Honecker? They talked, danced
apparatcheek-to-apparatcheek
(and kissed on the photo record mouth).

Stop, Look Up ... and Seal

Every time the cascading
contemptuous rhythm, *your
father's still perfecting ways
of making* ... bossed on through,
my boy-eyes went unhindered
to the ceiling – a kind of
lofty white ceiling would be it,
not too ornate, in need
of waxing, not that simple.
For decades whenever
the salutary lyric
tongue-lashed the girl my eyes
went up there till at last
a dab of possibility
and reason sealed a different
interpretation but
to this day should the sardonic
zeit music get played and
lay on me its jeering lines, I'm
stuck first and foremost on the ceiling.

Flection

The animal kingdom is riven
by a far-reaching disparity between
creatures that can't scratch their butt and those
that can, raccoons, monkeys and such.
(All the thinking which comes with
the ploy, territory. Corkscrews from it.)

Another divide, casts promising light:
between those females that stand
upright, I don't say stolid, to pee –
the rhino, the horse. And those that sink,
some deeper than some, on variably
posed legs, and could be heels for their part

tilting, easing up off the ground:
dogs, sheep, us. Even human males
have occasionally been disclosed in the distance
giving by road edge, tree, late night brick wall,
that brisk absent-minded little dip to
the knees, in the name of shake-and-zip.

Honest Years

Reading the lines of poems, like reading the lines
of palms (on first dates, in pubs), has gone out –
for the public at large, and socialized.

Nonetheless … kept on contentedly
paddling round the lobsterpots, buoys, lighthouses,
eyeing my early catch, mending my nets, when I'd been

right round a fair moment to start again. A friend
having formed two cautious scant piles, the likes and
the likes less, I was not against – by explaining stuff or

a repair, on the spot – causing a poem of mine
to flutter across, from their pile B to their
pile A (as in the Windows box which boasted

document copying, folder to airy folder …).
When an SAE came back thick, it was a death
warrant in my own handwriting. And if,

after ages in the warmth of cocooning belief,
flaws irremediable saw me brusquely in the
end withdraw respect, and coldly flick a text

onto *my* dispassionate B pile – a private
catastrophe for the poem, which went pale, would
never be approached with love again, or at all.

I shook from an envelope a stapling of mag-
rejected poems. With love not overly killed by *that*,
plonked them atop a squat bookcase. Doors re-opened,

the odd breeze. For days the uppermost page
an engrossing missive chanced on, lit on, then it hung
one afternoon by the staple, blankside down over

the face of the bookcase. Chuffed I called 'Wind's
on my second page!' (lightly puffing its p.1
fringe with concentration). I had, after all the years,

a real Deutschmark hoard of poems under
my mattress, and when I was good and ready
I took them to a bank. They said, '*Dead currency.*'

An All-Star Reception Er When

Present were stars from all walks and runs
and trots of sport and show in suits and
blazers fetched up against each other
in the rigours of bland conversation
flouted only by the high tones of the
clever tennis star *You cannot
be Sirius!* snubbing the dim
dog star and his opinions.

Within Reach

A tramp is somebody nobody
will ever listen to properly again.
Love, work, family, position:
all for accruing people to whom
we signify, who listen, who
have to listen and vice-versa.
But the impingeless essence of tramp.
That sober location-changing silent – in
hooded quilt-black – stoical thick-set
midlife tramp for one (a throwback,
see under homeless). Within reach
of the Thames, never seems to lift
his gaze, but can lower unfazed
his body to sleep with discipline
on day park benches.
                    To impinge:
all that U.S. grudge gun killers – campus,
mall and workplace multi-murderers
(suicide bombers without a cause
and with a meaningful kill-die delay) –
want before they go.
                    And impingement
eyes shut? Would be what the Scandinavian
girl singer was after, who leapt out rapt
onto the heads of the masses, the woven
mass of fans nearest the stage, for
the hallowed (rarer now) Crowd Surf, but
they sort of parted – instinct, not malice –
and she was injured quite seriously.

Comets Meteors Eras

The era
from Caruso to Carnera,
of the airy
voice and meaty aura.

In the century
since then only ten or
so meteor
-ite lump recoveries.

Draveil, Paris:
one of the meagre lumps plummet
through the roof, last year, of the
famille *Comette*.

Stranger Warmth

When you drive on round a sharpish bend locked
into a wide yawn and see nonetheless past
your yawn a car bearing down just like that:
vision in the raw, mortal threat on the quiet,
reality of an inflated grain. Your response
impassive as well as larger than life. Mainly
though, the narrow country lanes constitute

a matchless device for the manufacture
of good will here, nutshells of stranger warmth
not easily come by. The jockeying
tendency, to see who can pull over first
into a gateway and sit with measured
consideration, car-obscured, not oblivious
to the hand in the windscreen of passing thanks.

A satisfaction too – and unswerving ritual –
for the one raising it. State a hand, succinctly
loved after all, pulled over for. (At dusk
the protocol becomes: rapid double
flash for No You, Keep Oncoming *You*, and from the
beneficiary a single eloquent deal-
closing snap of fullbeam, the transience a skill).

Sometimes a lunge of variance. No bulge
you can spy in the lane or gate latitude
for you, on or back, but beyond and behind
them, yes discernible, not far. So bonnet-
to-bonnet posture, spot of mere stare to stare:
they have to reverse. After which they choose –
relying on imminent departure

never they reckon to meet again,
and on vehicular encasement all
except for the driverside window rolled down
in readiness – to *badmouth you almost
incomprehensible, and something rotten*
(as no way they would on foot, or in public).
To throw out – driver might even be, with private

schoolchild in back, a middle-aged woman possessed
of this extra-curricular persona – at
the right window-to-window moment eyes ahead:
seething rudeness like a bag of rubbish. Half-caught
lingering bag, shredding. As social gagtape
breakthrough shout opportunity not to
be missed, but are they saying they lose nothing?

Now descends the ...

Now descends the yellow toad,
now parachutes the red.
It's in the dewlap of the Gods.
And they have hesitated:
'The wheel is turning, but the hamster is dead.'

Far From How

The photos our hostess brought back to the table
so brightly, revealed me scumble-faced,
flaw-necked, and very far from how
I'd seen myself in that idyll, the summer
supper on a Norwegian housefield hillock
under fjord mountains, food trails across
the table woodgrain, meadow stems hooked
adorningly round a few of our ears

by the youngest of us. Then glum with zooming in
on the face (its value in freefall), I thumbed
upward across the entrusted phone screen (for
something, anything but), down to the chest.
Slightly fleshy, bared orange-mauve in the sun.
A perceptibly hairy surface parcel
of bleak 'charismatic megafauna',
orang-utan found conscious in beleaguered

verdant tatter. I asked our hostess might
I delete a photo or two. She sharply
refused. I murmured OK you keep
the copy, I'll delete the original.
And soon summarily receded
down the grassy hillock and unregarded up
pensive into the old Norwegian attic,
its air floorboard-clefts beams and ropes.

A Crab Steps In

Meagre waves curled onto the sand full of
flecks of seaweed, chopped up (by sea) and murking
the transparence like tea leaves. From the approach

track above, you could sight a large hornet
pinning down each ochre outcrop of brief
cliff that commanded a beach cove. White hornet

of motor home. It's believed jellyfish
may well inherit the polluted seas,
eventually jellyfish – already legion

in dodgy soupier bays of the globe.
A crab took its chance: stole somebody's
wristwatch as they bathed. Brandishing

the timepiece, went down a hole in the sand,
along a corridor, and placed it in the crab-
chamber, telling immured and neat around.

What's This?

I was so harshly woken by an agitated
barren phrase ill carved in the perfect tense.
Disgruntled shock and pain (and incredulity
stowed blackly aside): I dressed, went, climbed her too steep
for her stairs. The evening before – and our dropping by –
hadn't seen fit to dislodge any clue, but two clues
hunted down and a handbag were the last things I gave her
(the 'easy' crossword, no.2; and her bag rescued
after third party tip-off, from the walkframe with pouch
parked round the back in the rain-through dark). Halfway
between the bed and commode she lay in her white
nightie, legs drawn up to no purpose, skin going grey.
Her body a small, preposterous sheath
to have held a human, clinched a spirit.

999 as taught, as obliged, advising
turn her over, pump her chest, but I didn't
want to harass her (dead) shape. And a precision-
made tunnel, universal black within the Irish
pale blue of her one open eye, was lugging
at me to look down into the nothing (trained but
not impervious hands would soon be shutting off).
My mother's overnight escape from my mother
crushing. Across her cheek my finger, seeking to rest
and to mean, was set down parallel to the nose (its
stronger-than-supposed bridge, and mouth ajar rid of breath)
to stretch, if stretching to anything, behind the
stone of her death to the fleeing pool of warmth,
our warmth (specialized I confess not in touching
but joking.)
          The police, and the ambulancemen

who'd nudged her body back up, onto the bed, were now
downstairs. Non-joking coffee morning folk, there to greet
the undertakers.
      A day or more later, post-dawn,
I was almost sleeping, dozing drearily,
my organism, mechanism, anyway
a noise going in and out against the pillow,
corner task wheeze. The thinking with disgust, what sort
of cheap grotesque (audible side of dotted
line, *as* it happens) stay-alive bellows is this?

Our German Guest

Germany's era of nuclear fear ended with
Helmut Kohl in his sober broad-throated
cardigan, and Gorbachev in his zippered
blue cardigan, meeting in relaxed bare-headed
fashion for their own 'walk in the woods' of the Ukraine.
How could nuclear war and nuclear fear be halted
just by cardigans (even televised cardigans)?
- were her concise feelings as a teenager then.

Cry Of The No-No

The regular composition of short text
messages, WhatsAppings etc – rapid
thumb-tappery, and smooth lob to recipient –
signals competence in our society.
Regular composition of short texts

in lines however – *poems* – is a mark
of woeful judgement, incompetence.
Best not 'fessed up to at blithely mainstream
parties, and least of all to buoyant declared
denizens of the poetry ghetto,

verse-guanoed peripheral tower ... So when
it comes, 'And *what* do you write?', after
the saddened inner adumbration of the case
and forever disinclined mouthing of the clash
to answer, try 'something – small and cagey'.

Unless, that is, you're a Turner-Prized deadpan
cross-dresser who can with a steady eye offer
the interlocutor cups, or vases, scribbled
with story poems denaffeinated by *art*.
Despite all of which the occasional nuanced,

obdurate reading to your wife (who knows, gets
your eyes subtexted in red, and calls for why
not one or two say) 'helps with self-rimmage'...
A poem of huge seriousness and scope?
The phrase may yet find its way into the rare

fenced-off meek, for old times' sake waved through, Books
(Poetry) page. But for the rest of readership,
mingling alertly on the Fiction or History
pages, a present-day 'poem' (not writ on a
conceptual vase or in the empackaged shrunk

print, the word scroll laid back, of a CD's lyrics) –
a poem is *not* serious and has *no* scope,
by national not-stupid consent. Non-starter.
And duly not started, on tube or beach no no
not a line or a look-in. Poetry's disgracing

has effected a brazen inversion: 17th
century, First World War, Confessional, a poem
was by (donnish) definition 'more than the sum
of its parts'. Stuff it as you may now with handsome
insights, many or a few, and – *it's* (bye-bye) *less*.

Monochrome Gig

Amy Winehouse so different from all that
tabloid stuff about her, despite the 'mental hair',
declared the Irish organizer of the gig,
quiet gig, she did over there. I thought first of
an eddying outgrowth from Amy Winehouse's
brain (she – the Irish – was referring to).
Second of the facial hair the (documentary)
camera at the gig had seemed to welcome in
the foreground margin, and quarter profile, linger
by without remark, the dark wisps trending
down the rear of Amy Winehouse's cheek,
laudably unbeauticianed, laser-free,
not a preoccupation. And only lastly
of the ravenly bulked-up topheavy
sane and lurid courage of the hairdo.

Gamut

The hunting instinct has been largely reduced
to hunting for tidbits of trapped interdental
meat before bed. The (nanobrush) pokings, rich

or scanty. For a million years or whatever
our self-image was watery, done from beneath,
with bad perspective and prone to corrugation.

It might include a pop-out item which
presents the greatest distortion, contortion
from original – taste, food-shunting, tooth-cleaning,

temperature-regulating – function in the whole
gamut of animal history: this frantic tongue.
Robots may have voices, but we dare say never

will have tongues. Like Asimov (most advanced
of his day) some walked with bent legs, shuffling steps
in the manner of Chinese women with feet

bound in the past. The bolder-striding early robots
all (fretting boffin at their side) in practice
keeled over. But those bold strides, or phases, of *ōurs*. Will prove

four, tapering: *Natural, Manmade, Virtual, Extinct.*
Forest, city, cyberspace, and what cyberspace
is so absorbing and tactful a preparation for.

Over And Over Again

Entering sensorily the room in the dark
where she's long since bedclothed in sleep, I meet
as foreshadowed or not, with or without wince,
the foot of the bed with my knee, one line of the
imminent dim spread of a rectangle, and
set myself slewing probingly round the nearside
(verified) corner. Revolve onward, by dint
of weightless girths strung end to end, till my allotted
step-in, like tumbleweed goaded – by a wide
midwest American indie film wind – through
a puny exposed town low on people in the night.

Hoisted

Dreams the epitome
of 'too much information'.
But insomnia harbouring
worse, endgame of wordplay.
Better to be hoisted by –
bumped clear of the cliff –
your own Athos basket of sleep.

Jetties Out

A lamb of some substance up in the crook
of the field under a tall hedge, on
its flank. The legs' prominence and the sparse
neck movements, eked out. Dying over
two days perhaps, so 'calmly'
it impressed. But then calmness would spring
from dwindled and last brain function.
  ***

The shabby genteel section of
the minor Ston-to-peninsula road
touching down along a strip of north-east-
granted shore. And stone piles started out,
poking towards the sea in the likeness
of fallen-short jetties, knee-high,
metres from the road. Upon which
older people less well-to-do (the coast
there being rocky or dingy, less cued
to the sun, less appealing, and smacking
more of retirement to dwell in shacksize
sufficiencies) lay singly. Sunbathing
the most likely meaning of this,
although the sky muzzy. Neck movements
not observed, within the scrutiny
from cars of passage: they could be on ghats
(auspicious flamelets in the offing).
Or a slender glint of rollers, understood –
if coffinless in wait for the doors.
  ***

The full agony of what
death hands down, extinction horror,
reserved for middle years? The leading edge

of old age and the gather of diseases
sidling in, distract, get specific,
attenuate. Fray it along the way
to the final complicity? Some
condition is announced, terminal,
a fact of life, of timing, sombre
though natural. But that we *have* to die:
a fact of death, no sitting next to.

Scaredy Cusp

The Lambeth NHS clinic
psychological wellbeing
practitioners' cupboard, nook-stocked
with props and aids. Such as toy spiders
of rubber, faux fur, to help dispel
phobias, with humdrum fright

applied and re-applied. Concluding
stage, a real tarantula
on zoo release. The phobiacs
hold hands, the volunteer spider
joins in, puts up two, forms
the paramount link in the purging

circle, mouth parts solemn.
The zoo does expect a return
volunteer, a person newly soothed
to come, interweave and grace the ring
of spiders who've reported in, freaked mute
by (rainy weekend) cross-glass humans traipsing.

Virtuoso Drum Roll

I spat in a high wind and the spittle hung-
about-and-writhed, like a seagull or fighter jet
in evasive action. Travellers mention
the streets of Beijing being paved with saliva

not long ago (the pavements coated at least).
Something Muslims of 19th-century
Arabia were not supposed to
'willingly swallow', during daylight hours

of Ramadan. Inserted there, I would
have been pious, or pass unnoticed in China.
A cream-suited Englishman did pass
(away) unnoticed in Hong Kong – Denholm

Elliot, in a film. His third or fourth
and not wisest trip from home and wife,
nearing country retirement. Wreathed features,
decent, sensitive, rueful, taken ill

rumpled lengthways on the leather settee
of a club which by the Hong Kong 70s
had edged into out of place: white gloss, fine wooden
fittings, ceiling fans, beached Anglos. His heels –

insipid ankles, expensive English socks and
shoes – suddenly drummed the armrest at speed.
In sum, we swallow in the West
our spittle, in the East they eject it.

Incautious Pluck

Bending down steep to extract
an object partly overgrown
I was put to the indignity,
inappropriateness and pinpoint
outrage of being stung
by a nettle on my thinning patch.
Make that more thinning since
the nettle seems to have got
straight through to a sitting duck.

A king's crown may exactly fit,
encircle defend and conceal
a bald patch. Or woefully
demarcate expose and trumpet it,
you incautious in robes, stooping.

Anemone of the Evolved

Obama made his Climate Change speech which was key
before a pared-down invited (White House?) audience.
Top people, movers and shakers, several rows deep
round his apron of stage. Four out of five more intent –
back-row iPhones lofted clear of other top
shoulders – on the capture of him by their own (who
needs CNN) sheltered screens undeniably. Sure,
right there with The President, who struck his considered
(cheekbone-) angles. They stood at least looking his way,

not like those check-out-what's-behind-me selfie
adepts, who go crowd round celebs as ever
but *with backs turned,* so Facebook friends can savour
their friend's individuality of face, *plus* celeb
nameably bobbing somewhere in shot beyond,
bobbing with them shyly …
                                      After a Cretan beach
our return drive. Crossed the line of sun's immersing
gusted from out at sea. The few cars slackened pace
on the shelving quiet coast road: pullings over,

spillings out. Three or four people swung three, four
doors of a car halted in front. And materialized
with an aim, their mobiles already rising,
their arms like an anemone in a current
waving up in unison to snaffle the big
red orb sheathing down, into its pale grey shut-off.
Hardly a soul, along the road curves still warm,
was gazing at the sunset – not of the sun but
of this planet – except by (so evolved) phone.

Cow Motif

Replete udder thwacked (when the cow
really runs) up against one cowside
then the next, loud as a beaten carpet.
And – quite often by a field gate – the profound
concentric ripples, stormforce mudwaves dried
into a semi-mystery to set,

minor, beside corn circles. (Sheepwork?) Motif
recurring in the frown ripples sculpted
between and above cows' broad apart eyes.
As they frown placidly on. When *not*, but
coming at you, cows can be stopped dead
it's said with a stout intervention by

thumb and finger pinchlocking their nostrils,
not easy in the heat of a charge (though
a ruse matadors might try under
cover of a whirled cape). Unmoved
field bulls: the rough trade neck-hump, but also
thighs elegant raised and rounded.

Oscillatory

As you brush your teeth you may register
(but not perhaps within the mirror) a mild
clad jiggling of breasts or discreeter yet
of balls. Which kind of echoes (the dishwasher's
squeaky-clean wares having just been restored

to shelves, hooks) selected hanging mugs
caught on peripheral from the sink, high
and low, silently swaying all at the same
time. The last-hooked with some amplitude,
others less, others faintly … Right where

he juddered sweating in the loose pants
of his sheeny suit – the R&B frontman
on a jumped-up stage of the 'chill-in-circuit'
which wound fully black through halls, barns, backless
trucks of 50s America – she

reached up from the crowd, one prim heavy-built
sister in a trance, and patted him on the song.
Such was the bedlam and sexual arousal.
Then turned away with big eyes and
the archive depth of having done the due thing.

www.ingramcontent.com/pod-product-compliance
Lightning Source LLC
Chambersburg PA
CBHW032048290426
44110CB00012B/1001